Camps and Cottages

Camps
Cottages

········ A Stylish Blend of Old and New ··········

Molly Hyde English

Photographs by Linda Svendsen

Gibbs Smith, Publisher
Salt Lake City

First Paperback Edition
08 07 06 05 04   5 4 3 2 1
First Printed in hardcover edition in 2001 by Gibbs Smith, Publisher

Text copyright © 2001 by Molly Hyde English
Photographs copyright © 2001 by Linda Svendsen

Published by
Gibbs Smith, Publisher
P. O. Box 667
Layton, Utah 84041
Orders: (1-800) 748-5439
www.gibbs-smith.com

Designed and produced by FORTHGEAR, Inc.

Printed and bound in China

Library of Congress Cataloging-in-Publication Data
English, Molly Hyde.
         Camps and cottages : a stylish blend of old and new / by Molly Hyde
English ; photographs by Linda Svendsen. — 1st ed.
         p. cm.
      ISBN 1-58685-507-7
         1. Interior decoration—United States—History-20th century. 2.
Decoration and ornament, Rustic—United States. 3. Antiques in interior
decoration—United States. I. Svendsen, Linda, 1954- II. Title.
      NK2004 .E54 2001
      747—dc21
00-012251

Special thanks to the homeowners who graciously allowed us into their homes:

Judi and Luck Patterson
Joe and Carol Neil
Jim and Becky Clarke
Sidney and Jerry Muncy
Lynn and Monte Pries
Joe and Kathy Addiego
Rickie and Yank Sefton
John and Reo Haynes
Don Mahoney
Tim Lipinski
Wanda Westberg and Richard Pettler

This book is dedicated to my mother, Gladys Hyde, who taught me the meaning of grace and style, and to my father, John Hyde, who always reminded me that good things come to those who exercise patience and humility. It is also dedicated to the memory of Popeye, a wonderful cat who brought great joy and love to the Berkeley store. Abandoned, in ill health, emaciated and with feral instincts, he was truly a sight for sore eyes when we first found him. But with care, love and special treatment by one of Berkeley's most beloved vets, Dr. Charlie Berger at Campus Veterinary Clinic, we returned him to good health. For many years thereafter, the store and garden truly belonged to Popeye. So to him I say, "Godspeed little one. You will always be in my heart."

Acknowledgments

Though I am proud to have recaptured and rekindled interest in the design elements of what I believe to be a timeless style, I by no means take credit for the intelligent and intriguing ways in which the owners, whose living and work spaces have been captured in the book, have chosen to live. To a great extent, this is the story of their genius and creativity. I thank all of them for allowing me to work with lead photographer Linda Svendsen to capture the images that I believe reflect the essence of the Camps and Cottages style.

Gratitude to editor Suzanne Taylor for her initial interest, mentoring, and patience throughout the entire process.

Special acknowledgement and thanks to Candra Scott & Associates, Inc., including interior designer Richard Anderson and architect Herb Kosovitz. The photos found in the New England Colors section are the fine work of Dennis Welch, and the Lakeside Tradition shots are from the creative camera and eye of Holly Stickley. Thanks also to Tom Lamb for the kind use of his Laguna Beach studio.

All of us need to remember that dreams become reality not just as a result of hard work but also because of the care and unselfish grace of others. I wish to thank my angels—Tirzah Wanlass, Mary Emmerling, and Dianne Dorrans Saeks—for sharing my dreams with their readers and viewers and for providing me with reality checks along the way.

Though Steve Reed's designs are highlighted throughout the book, I can't begin to sufficiently acknowledge what his ideas, vision, and determination have meant to the development and success of the first Camps and Cottages store and garden. Thank you, Steve.

Thanks to Karen Stern for her perseverance and friendship, and to my brother, Frank, for his constant encouragement and guidance. Special thanks to Tony Perrott, who early on kept our Berkeley store shipshape.

Most especially I wish to thank my husband, Rich, who, along with our Labrador pups Hannah and Charlie, has provided me with the love and support to make dreams come true.

Contents

Childhood Dreams

It was during a family road trip from California to Colorado in the

summer of 1959 that I first came face to face with lodges, cabins,

and cottages. In retrospect, as I have grown my store, I like to

think of it as the first chapter in my long odyssey. President

Eisenhower's federal highway system— "the interstate"—was still

years away, leaving us with travel on the two-lane highways, or

what writer William Least Heat Moon later called "blue highways."

This kitchen, while rustic in appearance, contains
all of the modern conveniences, including a
compact counter for casual dining. Colorful
chinaware and a map tablecloth, popular during
the 1930s and 1940s, are personal favorites that
lend a cheery note to the overall cabin theme.

America
-Katherine Lee Bates, 1913

O beautiful for spacious skies,
For amber waves of grain,
For purple mountain majesties
Above thy fruited plain!

America! America!
God shed His grace on Thee,
And crown thy good with brotherhood
From sea to shining sea!

The adventure began just outside Los Angeles in the dairy town

my parents had called home since the depression. My father, a

hay-truck operator, took command of the family Chevrolet, and

my mother, an insurance-agency owner, assumed the role of

copilot and activities director. Heading east on what was then

Highway 66, all four of us, including my sister, Mary, made our

way past miles of orange groves in and around Riverside and

San Bernardino and stopped briefly to visit former neighbors

who had years before moved to the college town of Claremont.

It's a neighborhood that today remains home to shingled bun-

THERE IS
NO PLACE
LIKE HOME

Many textures and colors weave a playful
tapestry in this creative cottage room.

galows and quaint cottages designed by creative architects such as Charles and Henry Greene. The cottage was unforget-table—unlike the suburban sameness that had begun to overtake most of post-war Los Angeles, it was surrounded by fragrant roses, citrus trees, a picket fence, and large porch.

Reaching Arizona, we wound our way north on Highway 89 to Grand Canyon National Park, with a stop at the South Rim and

The Adirondack chair is a classic style. Though most are commonly painted in forest green, lodge red, sky blue, or white, an amber stain is a worthy option. It's not uncommon for someone, once attached to a chair, to not only maintain it for an entire lifetime but to proudly pass it on to sons and daughters.

the famous El Tovar Hotel. The canyon was the highlight for my sister

and me, but the lodge was special. Built nearly a half-century earlier by

the Santa Fe Railroad, it was the first structure of its kind that I had

ever seen. Perhaps it was due to my child's-eye view, but I remember

being overwhelmed. It was constructed of huge logs and stones that

looked as large as boulders. I recall how majestic it all seemed—espe-

cially the views through the lodge's picture windows—and we talked

about it all the way to Colorado.

We arrived in south-central Colorado at the Del Norte country house of

my Uncle Worth. Del Norte was then, and continues to be, a mining,

Cobalt blue walls provide a dreamy backdrop to a
room created by designer Becky Clarke. It is accented
with antique iron beds piled high with down-filled
comforters and colorful quilts. The unconventional
lamp, fashioned from a 1940s kitchen canister, adds
to the carefree feel of the room.

In a creative use of shelving, designer Becky Clarke incorporated a shelf across the entire length of the kitchen windows, creating the perfect display space for her collection of 1940s kitchen pottery.

ranching, and farming community on the Rio Grande River at

the foot of the San Juan Mountains. Worth, along with my

father, had packed peaches there in the summer of 1930 as

they made their way with most of their other ten siblings

from drought-stricken Holt, Texas, to a new life in California.

Worth liked it so much that he stayed—and with good reason.

It harbors a moderate climate and is a virtual mecca for hikers,

hunters, and fishermen.

The week was heavenly at "Camp Del Norte." We swam and

sunned along the nearby Rio Grande while the adults, parked

The powder room is reminiscent of what one might have found a century earlier in the captain's quarters of a majestic schooner.

in weathered metal lawn chairs (that today demand top dollar

at my store), exchanged family stories. Worth and my father,

both avid sportsmen, provided the entire clan with pan-fried

trout and other delights each evening while Aunt Irene saw to

it that the table was covered with plates of fruit and vegetables

picked daily from the local fields.

Tackle and gear were stored in a vintage hunting cabin just

down from the main house. The small, simple cabin was con-

structed of weathered boards. The inside walls were covered

with yellowing newspaper to prevent winter drafts. The cabin

A cozy living room, complete with an antique wood-
burning stove, is a blend of pine and vintage wicker.
A collection of porcelain hands, likely used years ago in
the manufacture of gloves, provides a creative accent.

Early-nineteenth-century photogravures by Edward S. Curtis are displayed within

unique leather and wood Craftsman frames and are tastefully accented by a floral

arrangement that is a brilliant contrast to the copper plates.

housed two metal bunk beds and, in the middle of the room, a wood-burning stove. There was no electricity or plumbing. Years later, Worth would tell me that, judging from the dates on the old newspapers on the wall, it had been constructed around 1915. Though it had at one point been deserted, he and his friends considered it their special retreat and breathed new life into the place.

I often look back at memories of that cabin and suspect that it was my first lesson in the meaning of style—that the oldest and most simply crafted furnishings represent what's best in all of us and can be used again and again with the right level of maintenance, love, and care.

At the house, evenings were spent outside under the light of vintage camp lamps and under the protective scent of citronella. The adults played cards, and we played hide-and-seek.

My recollections of that 1959 road trip—the sights, sounds,

scents and tastes—as well as the passing down of family

stories—-are as vivid as if they happened yesterday. The

mental snapshots are indelible, and I know that each garden,

cottage, cabin, and lodge I discovered on that trip represents

the earliest building blocks that eventually led to the Camps

and Cottages style.

The quilts on these shutter beds make a creative new use for collectible pennants. One encompasses East Coast and Midwest schools and locations, circa 1913, while the other focuses entirely upon California schools, circa 1915. The embroidered pennants are cross-stitched in a crazy-quilt manner, as was the fashion at the turn of the century. Between the beds, a night table is covered with a small circular quilt composed of about a dozen embroidered university banners, circa 1920. Rah-rah-rah!

·····The Road to Camps and Cottages·············

After college and careers in sales and marketing that took us to

Los Angeles, Denver, Houston, and San Diego, my husband and I

made career changes and moved to San Francisco, then eventu-

ally to the university town of Berkeley. Though my career

move was short-lived, it marked the beginning of life for more

than ten years in what the *New York Times* once called

America's "haven of renegade thought," and, most importantly,

put me on the path that would lead to the establishment of my

store, Camps and Cottages.

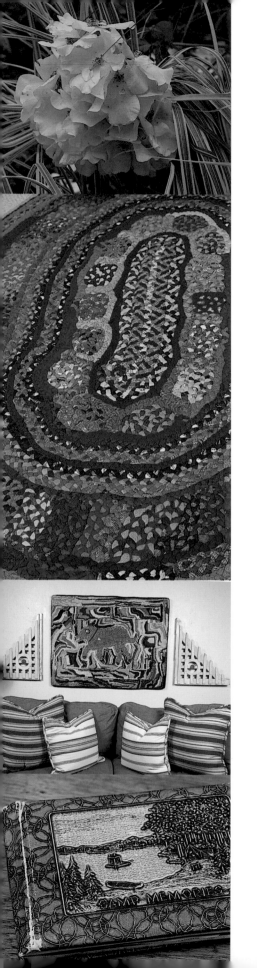

Life in Berkeley was unquestionably different. I soon learned that beyond the drumbeats of political marches and heated cultural debates quietly lay an intriguing and intelligent landscape of cottages, bungalows, and gardens. Though many of the structures had been neglected, at closer glance they all harbored the elements of grace, simplicity, and soul. To the credit of Berkeley's architectural as well as political activists, I was thankful that Berkeley's cottages had not, as a whole, been replaced by the bland and ill-scaled structures that had overtaken the rest of the California landscape. Furthermore, the foliage, though unkempt, had remained abundant, colorful, and in tune with the natural environment.

So it was that after months of searching we found refuge in a 1920s cottage. It was located in what is known as North Berkeley Hills, an area

Designer Sidney Muncy has taken bold steps in terms of color, texture, and statement pieces. Tucked between two vintage hooked rugs sporting dog motifs is a turn-of-the-century street clock from a country square in Connecticut.

Old Glory is appropriately positioned on an antler-adorned mirror matching the mirror in the dining room,

along with rustic walking sticks and a classic game of hearts. Though well connected to the outside world,

this retreat invites its guests to slow down and engage in the activities of times past.

that, before the turn of the century, had been platted by

Frederick Law Olmsted, the architect of New York's Central Park

and the principal landscape architect of the University of

California, Berkeley. It was our first experience with beveled-

glass doors, plaster walls, hardwood floors, and ceiling moldings

so grand that they seemed to assume a life of their own. We

reveled at the miniature octagonal tiles that had been set in the

bathroom and at the task of washing scores of panes embedded

within the sash throughout the house and French windows as

well as French doors. The tiny cottage consumed us, and we

dedicated ourselves to making it a warm and inviting retreat.

Little did we know that as we worked to tie the simple, sun-

filled colorful rooms, gardens, and furnishings together we were

engaging in what would become Camps and Cottages style.

"The use of color can be simple and dramatic," notes furniture craftsman Steven Reed. What better example than a sea-foam chair set against a white backdoor and the natural wood of the house—all accented by cascading impatiens in handcrafted window boxes.

Through the efforts of Bay Area environmentalist Stephen

Altschuler, author of a two-volume set on the hidden walkways

of Berkeley, and organizations such as the Berkeley

Architectural Heritage Association, we spent our early years hik-

ing, walking, and biking the town's lanes as well as touring its

gardens and homes. I discovered, much to my surprise, that

some of the most counterintuitive, eclectic, and fascinating

design ideas for both home and garden had been spawned not

during the 1960s but a full half-century earlier. The University

of California had attracted the world's most interesting people

long before the world had heard of People's Park, and those

early visitors brought new ideas in home design. The Tudor

*A quintessential camp bedroom with color
flowing from blankets, rugs, and the custom
wildlife lamp. The moose painting, a turn-
of-the-century realist piece, contrasts well
with the whimsy of the other furnishings.*

An old cottage, washed in barn red and accented with sea-foam green window frames, peeks through the overgrowth of the country garden.

An alcove just off this large kitchen houses a collection of 1940s cookware that designer Becky Clarke has

gathered over the years. Known for her creative use of color, she notes, "Nothing evokes the feel of my childhood

more than the colors, scents, and sounds of the kitchen, and for that reason I've always chosen to decorate my

living space with one or two colors pulled off an old map, linen, or vintage apron—colors you simply can't find

any longer."

© 2001 Maine Cottage
Furniture/Dennis Welch

homes with Asian gardens, Maybeck bungalows with stone floors, and brown-shingled cottages sur-

rounded by towering redwoods taught me that one could maintain simplicity, warmth, and tradition

while styling against the grain—an important premise underlying Camps and Cottages style.

By mid-1994, it was time to turn ideas and dreams into reality in the form of a store I named Camps

and Cottages. The store space needed to be sufficiently intimate, in a building with history, and in a

neighborhood with whimsy and unpredictability. I found just what I was looking for in an area north

of the University of California campus. It was a quaint neighborhood composed primarily of 1930s

homes and shops in what had been ground zero for revolution in the late 1960s, but which had

become Berkeley's "Gourmet Ghetto" when concerns for the palate displaced dreams of revolution.

Though the store has always been a work in progress, punctuated by zany characters and an eclectic inventory, by the second year I began to grasp the core ingredients that define the style. Perhaps as importantly, by that second year I had convinced the building's owner that the empty lot next door, a full 4,000 square feet, was worth more, financially and environmentally, as a year-round country garden than twice yearly as a pumpkin stand and Christmas-tree lot. With his concurrence, we created Berkeley's only country garden, complete with a handcrafted cabin and cottage constructed from the lumber of a century-old barn in nearby Napa Valley. The plantings were

This guest room is beautifully accented with a combination of new and vintage pillows from Country House Fabrics. The lamp is constructed of a 1950s beverage cooler and sits atop a twig stand—both are perfectly sized for the compact space.

specifically selected by Steve Reed and Don Mahoney, a botanist with the Strybing Arboretum in San Francisco's Golden Gate Park, to create a haven for birds and butterflies. It was spectacularly successful and quickly became a point of interest for town visitors.

The garden provided an idyllic setting for home furnishings under the watchful eye of a feral cat named Popeye, who appeared at our door in a terrible state but who was nursed back to health and remained the store's mascot for many years. Respect and love for animals is an important premise underlying the style.

In early 2000, I decided to expand Camps and Cottages to the 1920s southern California artists' town of Laguna Beach. Like Berkeley, it is rich in history and known for its blend of eclectic seaside cottages and zany activists. For all of the reasons we selected Berkeley, we are confident that Camps and Cottages will quickly become part of the Laguna landscape.

We hope readers will be inspired to add a touch of whimsy to their homes and that the Camps and Cottages style will be woven into homes across America, creating a truly new American style.

The Jasper sofa, piped in white over China blue for maximum drama and a vintage look, is one of designer Carol Bass's favorites. It provides a comfortable setting on the covered porch with a spectacular view of the lake.

Camps & Cottages

·····There's No Place Like Home·················

In the design and retail landscape of twenty-first-century

America—an environment that has been homogenized by the

growth of malls, big-box retailers, and online auction

houses—the two biggest compliments an independent shop

owner can receive is a new customer's notable pause upon

entering the store, followed by the cry, "I love what you're

doing here, but I can't put my finger on what it is!" Without

knowing it, that guest has just pierced the veil of daily

routine and entered the realm of style. It can't be

At the Idaho cabin of Becky and Shorty Clarke,
colorful wicker blends with Navajo designs to sur-
round a vintage camp table that is etched with the
names of young camp guests spanning forty years.

An Adirondack chair is a
comfortable and colorful addition
to the cottage garden.

bought, copied, borrowed, or imposed and is usually found

in small doses as well as in out-of-the-way places. It may take

the form of a new angle on an old concept, or the breathing

of new life into the discarded and forgotten. It is not to be

mistaken for a vacuous "trend," composed of discardable

look-alikes and knockoffs. True style is composed of an

indefinable mixture of ingredients—some planned and some

unplanned, some new and some old—but all of which lend

themselves to personal expressions that are unique,

memorable, and timeless.

Hints of bed-and-breakfast adorn the walls of this vintage cottage. Its pink patina creates a distinct connection between the cottages of Cape Cod and those of southern California.

Camps and Cottages style explores a host of distinctly American cottages that represent a combination of rustic and casual living, with particular emphasis upon the elements of color, dimension, and decorative whimsy. Its inspiration is a combination of the rustic living style so prevalent prior to World War I and of a more casual style that exploded onto the scene in the 1930s and 1940s, emphasizing excitement, color, and whimsical seaside living. It is cozy and truly American.

Though the coolness of white may have ruled the 1990s, today's look is dedicated to color, using it as a tool of expression as well as a source of energy.

The entryway to Camps and Cottages' country garden is entwined with the vines of colorful passion fruit. The contrast with the century-old brown shingle lends age and tradition to the urban garden.

Color

Camps and Cottages style focuses upon color. The homes and furnishings that follow exhibit the form and function of true-blue American style energized with the colors and movement of coastal environments—what award-winning Bay Area–craftsman Steven Reed calls "the incorporation of eclectic boldness with the honesty and vitality of heartland tradition." Traditional Americana style, with its emphasis upon maple woodwork, primary-colored textiles, muted pewter work, and the shadows of serious portraiture, continues to be beloved by many for its consistent, loyal, and conservative portrayal of early America. Camps and Cottages maintains a respect for this while introducing the use of vivid hues as a source of design energy.

Color and whimsy are the focus of this residential backyard garden. The use of cutouts, predominantly from the 1940s and 1950s, reminds one how colorful and creative garden design can be.

Handcrafted souvenir canoes, totems, baskets, and other artifacts depicting
Native American life have always adorned lakeside cottages and cabins.

Camps and Cottages was further inspired by a handful of artists who, after having been trained in the salons of the eastern seaboard and Europe, immigrated to California to capture the colors, lighting, and shapes of its countryside. Viewed then as nonconformists, these plein air artists focused upon an impressionistic view of the western landscape, representing a departure from the realist school that is most closely associated with Americana. As Jean Stern, executive director of the Irvine Museum, noted, "California's rich topography, year-round temperate climate, and perennial sunshine made it a haven for the landscape painters, and others who were primarily figure and portrait painters soon succumbed to the lure of the landscape. Rich and varied color was seen year-round, ranging from the many earth tones—greens, yellows, browns, and reds—to elegant blues and purples."[1]

Turn-of-the-century forged-iron doorstops depicting cabins, flowers, and seascapes provide a memorable way in which to open up the smallest cottages and cabins to indoor/outdoor living.

Where true Americana focuses upon forest greens, Camps and Cottages style captures interiors and furnishings in a variety of greens, from sea foam to eucalyptus and sage. Not only do the colors evoke a new sense of energy, but for the imaginative decorator they also release memories of the fragrances that are indigenous to the seashore and trails. Similarly, where true-blue American focuses upon the tradition found in delft and royal blues, Camps and Cottages seeks to capture the whimsy and drama of the sea by using cobalt, indigo, and navy. Perhaps the most dramatic uses of color are of red and yellow and their variants, all inspired by the magnificent sunsets that grace the deserts year-round and the coast during the warm days of mid-autumn.

These embroidered tourist pillows make bold statements when placed against the gingham upholstery. The use of antlers, both above the fireplace and in the dining room chandelier, give the room campy appeal. The red shutters bordering the river-rock fireplace are a unique way to complete the hearth.

Cottage furnishings add dimension and personality to this garden.

Dimension

Transforming a modern living space into a cottage may seem like a formidable task, but one of the biggest obstacles is mind-set—challenging convention and stepping outside the white box. Another concept is the introduction of dimension and texture. Though few are as bold and creative as Becky Clarke—a McCall, Idaho-based stylist and storeowner who has magically transformed suburban homes in California, Oregon, and Montana into spectacular cottages—transition can be as simple as the addition of country shelving throughout the space or the construction of ledges and mantels. The style calls for unfettered dimension and texture. An example of this is seen in the use of hardwood floors, where a timeworn surface is preferable to a perfect finish. Though proportion is important, there can never be enough chairs in a vintage cottage or cabin. Even though a seating base is established around a matching fabric, an eclectic mix of chairs made up of fabric, wood, and vintage leather, though appearing at first to be mismatched, will soon be appreciated for their counterintuitive beauty.

Complementing a well-worn mix of club chairs is a colorful arrangement of vintage or handcrafted benches. Liberal use of dissimilar benches, some housing pillows near a wall or spaced at odd angles near sofas and chairs, provides every cottage and cabin with a lived-in feeling. Vintage or handcrafted shutters, corbels, molding, and related architectural pieces in their original and weatherworn condition provide timeless texture to walls, corners, and window frames. They also represent an intelligent and clever way to upgrade otherwise lifeless covenants that restrict outside makeovers in today's planned communities.

Designer Becky Clarke's close friends Mary and Sandy Carter live a few miles away; their place, which decades ago was a livestock birthing barn, reflects the log-cabin look with an old stove and fireplace. The Carters have filled their home with flowers housed in colorful New England sap buckets.

·····Decorative Whimsy···

The art of whimsical appointment begins with objects closely

linked to family. Family photographs, books, silverware, and

china are givens. But whimsy goes a step beyond, focusing upon

the obvious as well as the not-so-obvious: a fifty-year-old baby

rocker situated atop an eight-foot-tall carved-out closet; a Maine

black bear, from the region in which the homeowner was raised,

mounted in 1939; a grandfather's boating trophies; skookum

dolls; vintage sock monkeys; or a Pennsylvania-pine bookshelf

topped by a Hawaiian rattan lamp from the early 1940s. The

possibilities of fusing cultures and time periods are unending.

Whether one is an owner of a centuries-old cottage or a decorator

planning the makeover of a client's modern home, all at some point

seek to identify and establish historic ties and soulful elements that

work to complement country colors and creative dimensions. The vin-

tage photographs and sketches found in some of the great cottage and

cabin books—including William P. Comstock's *Bungalows, Camps and

Mountain Houses,* published in 1915; William S. Wicks's *Log Cabins

and Cottages,* originally published in 1920 and republished by

Gibbs Smith, Publisher, in 1999; as well as F. E. Brimmer's *Camps,

Log Cabins, Lodges and Club Houses,* published in 1925—can

also provide inspiration.

*By creatively using textured tin, bead board,
exposed shelving, and oak flooring, architect
Lynn Pries gave this kitchen a facelift, making it
enviable for any country home.*

This courtyard is accented with a time-worn bench and a
collection of colorful watering cans.

Join us as we explore vignettes in New England, mid-America,

the Rockies, and the Pacific Coast for fresh cottage ideas,

including an eclectic display of early-twentieth-century

California and American folk art, colorful and solidly crafted

furniture, textiles and vintage collections—all of which come

together in the Camps and Cottages style.

*Awash with ivy-covered walls, bold
English colors, and scores of roses,
this cottage sits within the shadows
of aromatic eucalyptus trees.*

[1]Stern, Jean Dominik, Janet Blake, and Harvey
L. Jones. *Selections from the Irvine Museum.*
Irvine, California: The Irvine Museum, 1992.

Rustic

Utter the words rustic or retreat and you're immediately reminded of the outdoor vistas of the great camps of the Adirondacks, the summer homes along New York's Finger Lakes, the spectacular estates along the banks of Lake Michigan, and the vintage retreats nestled around Colorado's Grand Lake. Those outdoor vistas, though magnificent, are in many respects nothing more than entryways to the true soul of rustic living captured within indoor living spaces.

At Lake of the Woods Mountain Lodge and Resort, man's best friend greets visitors to this general store—stocked with all the staples and equipment needed for a classic day on the lake. The camp baskets on the porch can be a great addition to any camp or cottage, and the colorful megaphones are instant reminders of a simpler time.

A vintage radio is a nostalgic bedside companion in this rustic room setting.

Unlike their light and airy cottage cousins, rustic retreats have,

at times, been characterized as overly masculine. Though the

observations and criticisms about this may raise emotions

among purists, they are fair. As a result, women have begun to

make an impact and difference in the design and development

of rustic spaces by utilizing the colorful tones of Camps and

Cottages style. Alone or in collaboration with male colleagues,

today's designers and owners have begun to envision and

construct rustic living spaces that capture a robust sense of

history and tradition while introducing bold colors, unusual

dimensions, and a strong decorative base.

Layers of beacon bay, plaid, and canvas-covered pillows lend colorful contrast to the down-filled duvet and hickory bench, which doubles as a bed stand and sitting area. The bookcases on each side of the bed are one of many space-saving techniques employed by cottage designers and reflect the Arts & Crafts style.

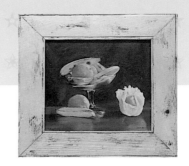

Lakeside Tradition

Leading the pack among designers who have taken on the

challenges of creating a rustic retreat in the style of Camps

and Cottages is San Francisco's Candra Scott, of Candra Scott

& Associates. Along with colleague Richard Anderson, she has

redecorated the Lake of the Woods Mountain Lodge and

Resort in Klamath Falls, Oregon. Tucked within the Siskiyou

Mountain Range in southern Oregon, the magnificent twelve-

cabin lodge has been situated on the banks of its namesake

lake since the early 1920s and includes a general store and

marina that continue to serve residents and visitors.

The resort was originally constructed as a fishing retreat. Great care was taken by its original builders to situate each structure in a fashion that does not disturb or detract from the beauty of the lake. The oldest existing structure is the general store, dating to 1924. The lodge's lobby is characteristic of the forests surrounding the property, including walls covered in knotty pine and antlers and trophies commemorating hunting days gone by. The picture windows reflect magnificent lake and forest vistas. A vintage WPA-era mural depicting American Indians in canoes adorns one of the walls, and, when combined with the period's ceiling fans and antler lighting, it creates a spirit of wilderness, casual elegance, and comfort. The staff members are even attired in shirts manufactured by the state's premier Pendleton Woolen Mills.

The whimsy of flowers in a vintage cooler plays well against the massive display of river rock, turning this lodge room into an inviting retreat. The accents include a wildlife trophy, bear rug, and overstuffed chairs. Although new leather chairs are in vogue, they rarely match the patina and feel of vintage pieces. Search for leather chairs from the 1930s, even if unmatched. A seasoned upholsterer can easily refurbish the underlying frames and padding, giving them a second life for your cottage or home.

Spectacular red and amber hues make this lakeside lodge room a special destination for the reader who has brought a favorite book to camp. An example of the classic rustic look, the room illustrates how homeowners may transform favorite reading rooms into rustic retreats by adding modest touches. Camp lamps, composed of twigs or portions of an animal trophy, lend great character and warmth.

A 1940s kitchen with green-and-white-checked tile contrasts the adjoining room's golden knotty-pine walls. The table is adorned with an original heavy cotton tablecloth from the 1930s. Though original tablecloths are becoming more difficult to find, especially those with manufacturer tags still intact, they are a bright and playful kitchen addition. The colorfast motifs range from fruits and vegetables to floral prints and tourist roadmaps.

The cabins are brown clapboard with green roofs; red front doors and window boxes adorn each structure. Each cabin contains a potbellied stove, and the ticking and floral-draped window treatments frame windows that provide unimpeded views of the lake. Walls of honey-colored knotty pine are covered with original art that has been collected locally. In the cozy sitting area of each cabin is an eclectic mixture of vintage and hand-painted furniture.

The marina contains a dockside tackle shop and supplies veterans as well as first-timers with state-of-the-art fishing equipment. A special feature is its display of vintage lures, poles, and reels, providing the angler with a sense of historical connection to the property. Its deck is lined with Adirondack chairs and picnic tables perfectly situated for resting, reading, and lunching at the lake's edge.

The resort, though filled with the latest guest amenities, is a

place where families and friends connect past and present.

Redwood Roadhouse

As one of America's most creative innkeepers, Margaret Grade,

of Manka's Inverness Lodge, has maintained tradition while

incorporating her own design touches to produce what

Frommer's calls a ". . . lovable old hunting lodge . . . one of

our favorite places to stay and dine on the [California] coast."

As Grade describes it, the heart of Manka's is a 1917 hunting

and fishing lodge in the elegantly rustic and simple California

A turn-of-the-century tub highlights this
crisp-looking bathroom, accented with an
original physician's cabinet and vintage coat
rack, all in white. The painted charcoal floor
is brightened by the use of border trim.

This comfortable nook is the perfect place to play a game. This is a fun example of boards that were sold between 1900 and 1940 that were designed so many games could be played on them.

Arts & Crafts movement. It sits about an hour north of San Francisco, with Tomales Bay at its feet and

the Pacific Ocean at its back. In addition to the main lodge there are other guest quarters, including

cabins, a beach cottage, and a boathouse, all of which have been carefully maintained and decorated by

Grade to reflect the Arts & Crafts tradition while remaining true to the strength and wildness of the

northern California seashore and countryside.

The two cabins on the grounds were built in 1900. The more indulgent of the two is Manka's Cabin, a

two-room structure with a massive fireplace, a vintage two-person tub, and a shower that opens to the

sky. The Fishing Cabin has an ocean-rock fireplace and similar tub. The beach cottage overlooks

Tomales Bay and is tucked into two private acres at water's edge. It was built in the 1850s as a hunting cabin and is beautifully furnished with Arts & Crafts pieces,

overstuffed down and feather chairs, and a wood-burning fire-

place in the living room. The 1911 boathouse is a dramatic

two-unit structure built directly over Tomales Bay. In matters

of design, dimension, tradition, and upkeep, Manka's epitomizes

the history and tradition of the Camps and Cottages style.

722 LB. TUNA

Globes were an especially prized item between 1910 and 1945 as they enabled radio listeners to trace the adventures of arctic explorers and globe-hopping pilots, as well as the movements of clashing forces during two world wars. Today they make welcome accents to place alongside trophies from the same period, the most valued of which represent the achievements of family members.

This bench has a lift-up seat for the storage of blankets, and its blue hue adds camp style to the weathered exterior of the original cistern.

Harbor Lights

Recently designated by the respected Berkeley Architectural

Heritage Association as a historically significant structure, this

century-old "brown shingle" sits within the heart of what Bay

Area architectural historians characterize as Maybeck country,

high in the Berkeley hills with uninterrupted views of San

Francisco, the Golden Gate Bridge, and the entire bay. Shortly

after purchasing the property, Carol and Joe Neil researched its

history in preparation for restoration. Constructed at the turn

of the nineteenth century by a Swedish immigrant and family

farmer, and being one of only a handful of original rustic

structures that survived the great Berkeley fire of September 1923, it anchors an area that was platted by Frederick Law Olmsted. With its stunningly simple sense of dimension, Harbor Lights is adorned with uncomplicated colors true to the era. Besides the main residence, the compound includes a guest home as well as the original cistern housed in its own building, which, after more than a century, continues to feed the multileveled landscape with freshly chilled creeks and waterfalls originating from the underground waterways that lace the Berkeley hills.

Accented with a shade of green reminiscent of the great camps of the Adirondacks, this early century brown shingle sits on an acre of hillside property and is surrounded by foliage. The covered porch is filled with turn-of-the-century wicker furniture.

The surrounding property of this cottage has been enhanced with sublevels of foliage fed by water from an underground cistern. It is an excellent illustration of a well-cared-for garden that provides the natural look and flow synonymous with rustic retreats and simple cottages.

The house, once the centerpiece of a late-nineteenth-century working farm, is accented with a host of original farm pieces including this wheelbarrow. The pieces are filled with the bounty unique to each season and provide colorful and historical accents to the area.

The antler-adorned mirror adds just the right hint of "the hunt" to the finely detailed dining chairs. The use of leafy twigs accented with pyracantha softens the masculine presence of Black Forest furniture.

Northwoods Manor

It's a long way between the owners' San Francisco Victorian

perched among companion estates in the Pacific Heights sec-

tion of that city and their 125-acre redwood retreat. Where one

exudes historic and high-end style, the other provides a down-

to-earth feel that is both rustic and luxurious, thanks to the

architectural magic of Herb Kosovitz and the design genius of

Candra Scott and Richard Anderson. The compound, tucked

entirely within a grove of redwood trees, is composed of the

main house—wherein most of the family activities are

focused—a guest house, two cottages, a bandstand, a theater,

and a pool with a pool house.

The genius of this room's design stems from the dissimilarity of its furnishings. From asymmetrical mica shades and canoe accents to contrasting sofas and a Chinese lantern, this room represents a layering of tastes and cultures.

Originally constructed in the 1960s in a style best described as

"California Country Shingle," architect Kosovitz was faced with

transforming an otherwise uninspired living space into a

retreat imbued with the classic characteristics of the 1930s.

He opened up a series of small rooms to create a single grand

living area, including entry, living room, and dining room. A

game room was constructed on the second level. The ceiling

was lowered and a large stone fireplace was constructed as the

living room's focal point. Walls of ungainly sheetrock were

refaced with handcrafted planks from fallen redwood trees

found on the property. The 1960s kitchen was transformed

into a vintage masterpiece complete with features and

appliances required by today's gourmet chefs.

The creative use of logs completes the furnishings in this rustic game room. A large canvas-and-leather steamer trunk from the 1930s is stacked with colorful trade blankets.

In dramatic and airy contrast to the rustic formality displayed throughout the rest of the house, this kitchen is colorful and camp-like, using a shade of green similar to what might have been found in a 1930s tablecloth. Whimsical hooked rugs warm the Etruscan tile, and the display of camp baskets creates the perfect separation between window panels.

With structural refurbishment completed, the owners turned to Scott and Anderson for the interior.

Their design team developed a theme that combines elements of European Black Forest, Adirondack,

and early Rancho California. After designing the custom-upholstered pieces, Anderson scoured the best

of the local flea markets as well as his favorite purveyors of American furniture and crafts, accumulating

just the right collection of vintage items. These included a collection of American Indian rugs, naive

paintings, and vintage Beacon blankets, as well as Pendleton camp and trade blankets. Scott's acquisi-

tions from a buying trip to Paris—Black Forest pieces, leather club chairs, and French tramp art—were

unique additions that proved more than adequate to anchor a magnificent makeover. The owners took

part in the hunt with their own addition of a superb nineteenth-century Black Forest gun case and a

rare vintage sixteen-foot wooden canoe. The designers also worked with a private source in the design and manufacture of vintage rustic western furniture from tables to bookshelves, including a number of theme variations developed specifically for this client. Sconces derived from an original 1930s art deco American Indian headdress highlight the interior. Oriental carpets and a dining table that once graced Hearst Castle were moved from the city estate to the country compound. And, with what the owners described as a stroke of genius, the designers introduced a pair of Chinese lanterns, reflecting the mania for Orientalist motifs so prevalent at the turn of the nineteenth century.

Camp lighting in this cottage remains on throughout most of the day to brighten the rooms, which are completely surrounded by forest.

The rich amber hue of a lacquered pine wallboard provides a classic look for the master bedroom in this log cabin. Two creative treatments of traditionally outdoor accessories are found in the application of weathered shutters to the inside of the house and the conversion of an old birdbath into a beautiful bedside table.

····· Country Roads ·····································

Tucked within the shadows of Brundage Mountain, just up the

road from Idaho's Payette Lake and near the resort town of

McCall, sits the latest rustic retreat of Becky and Jim ("Shorty")

Clarke. Clarke, known for her masterful makeovers and styling

of vintage cottages and homes in Oregon and California,

created a country roadhouse that explodes with color, warmth,

and whimsy, and that represents the clearest expression of the

Camps and Cottages style. Having inherited a neutral canvas,

she transformed each room into a unique living space through

the use of bold colors and vintage accessories.

She fused cowboy with American Indian and blended them with reminders of the area's golden years, beginning in 1920, when the logging community received its first winter visit from some of America's earliest downhill and cross-country ski pioneers. Those visits eventually led to the reestablishment of McCall as one of America's premier resort areas.

Located just outside the main house are two additional living spaces used by the Clarkes as guest rooms during the summer season—one an old camp trailer, complete with an advertisement for Becky's McCall store WaterLemon, and the other a completely furnished tepee. With such unsurpassed talent, it is not surprising that Clarke remains in constant demand as a design consultant to McCall's newest arrivals as they seek to unleash and accentuate the unique characteristics that make up their newly acquired lodges and cabins.

"We wanted to set a rustic tone at the front door and decided upon a deep-chocolate-brown framed-log design accented by the dramatic forest green of the door, shutters, and window frames. We think it has worked very well," says designer Becky Clarke. "You know for sure that you're not in Kansas anymore!"

With a traditional fire pit to keep it warm during cool nights, the tepee is decorated with twin beds, old stools, a camp table, a lantern, and vintage American Indian rugs.

From a cultural and historical perspective, the importance of the tepee cannot be overstated. From a design perspective, it represents Native American simplicity and genius at its best. We are happy to have recaptured the Native American spirit in the design and construction of this space," says Becky.

Country

In 1996 Camps and Cottages embarked upon a noble experiment with the conversion of a long-time-empty urban lot into a significant and special country garden. The 4,000-square-foot site next to the store had once been home to a laundry that was destroyed years earlier in a fire. Where neighbors saw a blighted tract, I envisioned a lush and natural country garden. With some timely coaxing of the parcel's owner, and assurances to a number of Berkeley neighbors known for their mastery of observance as well as unsolicited comments, the

This vintage cabin, constructed by Camps and Cottages, is overgrown with blossoming potato vines, adorned with an early-twentieth-century canoe on the roof, and appointed with classic wicker. "I don't know how many times I've been tempted to move in to this wonderful space, if even for a day, just to appreciate the beauty of the adjoining garden," says Steve Reed, one of the garden's principal architects.

Color stems from the impatiens planted in a coal bucket.

project moved ahead with the construction of a vintage cabin

and an artist's cottage from century-old recycled barn wood

found in nearby Sonoma County. The structures were

constructed by Connecticut transplant Jon Westberg, who, by

that time, had established himself as a well-known craftsman

of recycled rustic furniture and birdhouses.

The garden was concerved, designed, and developed as a bird

and butterfly habitat by Steve Reed, incorporating the genius of

San Francisco botanist Don Mahoney. Though the garden is

now being

"When planting a natural country garden, a principal focus should be on establishing a sanctuary for birds and butterflies," says noted botanist Don Mahoney. "The introduction of one of many available 'butterfly plants' will get you started,"

disassembled to make way for the development of a commercial and residential structure, its presence over four years made a significant impact upon all of those who visited, whether in conjunction with the Camps and Cottages store or simply to meditate on a vintage bench in what was certainly one of Berkeley's true urban oases. Just as importantly, it provided inspiration to all of those interested in converting empty space—no matter the size—into a living and natural garden.

The serendipitous cutouts of this planter along with its bold periwinkle blue wash make it a favorite.

Consistent with the Camps and Cottages style, Mahoney's approach is to nurture what is genuine. He has suggested the following guidelines for establishing and maintaining a wildlife garden:

■ Think diversity. Choose species that flower and fruit at different times of the year. With carefully chosen plantings, pollen and nectar as well as seeds and fruits will always be available for the proper nourishment of garden "guests" and sustenance of the garden itself.

Colorful mallow from the hollyhock family blends together with natural grasses to line a garden path.

Every garden should have a small area devoted to the storage of tools and the repair of artifacts.

A 1930s Radio Flyer wagon provides a
unique setting for pots of autumn marigolds
at the entrance of an open-air porch
accented by an iron bed from the
same period.

Remnants from a 1930s picket fence are sprinkled throughout the garden to add accent and character. They are enveloped by a combination of native grasses and a stand of Sally Holmes roses, both great staples in cottage landscaping.

■ Be sure to include a number of deciduous plants. Their yearly abundance of tender new growth and decaying plant parts provides sustenance for a variety of creatures. Many fast-growing plants and abundant fruit bearers fit within this class. Include perennial grasses, as they provide shelter and hunting grounds for insects and birds.

■ Think insects. You may resist the thought, but remember that a variety of backyard wildlife species rely significantly, and even exclusively, upon insects as their source of food. Begin taking more careful note of them and you will find that insects and

A fifty-year-old metal chair and table, tucked into a hidden corner of the garden, provide a perfect setting for reading, journaling, or taking afternoon tea.

other invertebrates can be among the chief delights in your wildlife garden.

■ Think insects again. Insects are the balance in the phrase "balance of nature." Predator insects such as spiders and ladybugs need a supply of food. Pesticide usage destroys the food chain and actually encourages outbreaks of the pests that predators might otherwise control. Avoid using pesticides wherever and whenever possible.

The twig settee looks invitingly comfortable under a stitched forty-eight-star version of Old Glory, all tucked within a rustic garden cottage. Sitting atop the desk is a 1930s Popsicle-stick lamp. The construction of Popsicle-stick items and matchstick boxes was a popular pastime at lakeside cabins and seaside cottages.

Two spectacular pieces, both late-nineteenth-century creations of the Lloyd Loom Company, grace the interior of the garden cabin and are accented with a hanging hooked rug. The table lamps have rawhide shades and leather stitching.

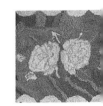

- Think natives. Local native plants are best adapted to your local climate. In northern California, for example, most of the native plants are drought-tolerant and are the best fit for a wildlife garden. They support not only local native insects but also the mushroom populations that have developed over thousands of years. And remember, it is not only in the tropics where native plants and animals are becoming extinct. They need your help, right in your own gardening space. You can make a global difference by acting on a local level.

- Keep artificial feeding of wildlife to a minimum. Concentrate on working to improve and expand the "carrying capacity" of your gardening domain. A balance will be struck.

The wood-chip path leading up to this cottage is lined with native grasses, and the cottage roof is enveloped with Chilean white passionflowers. Recycled chips were easily obtained from a tree-trimming crew that was willing to dump its loads at the garden rather than waste them at the landfill. Chips cool the garden—particularly after a watering or rainstorm—act as a natural deterrent for unwanted weeds, and provide a fresh and robust aroma for months. As the chips break down, they can be replenished. The beginning of each growing season is a good time to do this.

■ Water features are invaluable in wildlife gardens. We need the "pioneer" plants to work hand in hand with aquatic habitat gardening.

■ Monitor existing plantings before you decide to change plant species in a wildlife garden. Remember that the existing plants may have become a food or shelter source relied upon by wildlife—whether permanent or migratory. Plant a substitute prior to making the change.

Native California dune grasses interwoven with bronze honeysuckle and purple salvia frame the garden bench.

■ Finally, always feel free to make a note or two in a small notepad with your observations of the plants and wildlife—what has developed, what has not, and how the plants and wildlife are interacting—season by season. You will become one with your garden—a steward overseeing the welfare of delicate plants, fragile insects, and tender wildlife.

Roses, salvia, grasses, and honeysuckle
provide the eclectic framing of garden paths.

Cottage

The elements that make up a cottage can be seen in the

character of materials; respect for the past; simple, humble

lines; and the bold radiating colors that comprise them. It was

not until I began construction of the vintage structures in my

store's country garden that I focused upon the elements of

cottage comforts, beginning with the basic building materials.

Since a cottage is defined not solely by its age but also by its

character, I wanted to capture the passage of time. That desire

took me, along with builder and craftsman Jon Westberg, on

The likenesses of dogs are tastefully spread throughout designer Sidney Muncy's home in paintings, rugs, vintage cast-iron items, and painted statuaries, lending a personal country accent.

This whimsical living room is filled with vintage pond boats and great color. The unusually shaped antique wicker chair was actually included on the set for the 1988 motion picture Beaches.

a hunt throughout the rural countryside north of San

Francisco. The area is replete with old structures dating from

the late-nineteenth century. To the credit of preservationists,

even the most rundown and empty farms, poultry buildings,

and grazing structures must be left intact until nature and time

have leveled them. After several weeks, we came upon

remnants of a time-leveled barn in Sonoma County and, with

permission of the landowner, moved the lumber—just enough

for the small artist's cottage on the front cover of this book and

a one-room cabin back to Berkeley. Close examination of the

wood revealed an explosion of textures and colors.

P. I. BITNER, MEAT MARKET.

MENU

FRIED HAM AND EGG SANDWICH 2
FRIED HAM 15
WESTERN 15
TONGUE 15
SARDINE 15
CHOPPED HAM 11
SLICED HAM 11
CORNED BEEF 11
EGG 11
TRILBY 11
HOT ROAST BEEF 21
FRANKFURT 21

In daring design moves, designer Sidney Muncy and her husband replaced the "stock" kitchen floor with brick and mortar and refaced the kitchen walls with bead board to create a true-blue country look. Notice the gigantic rolling pin above the patio door and the sandwich sign, both unique advertising pieces recovered from a now-defunct Nebraska bakery.

Microscopic creatures had at some point called the lumber

home, and although the wood was dry when we found it, the

traces of the creatures' earlier presence left the wood with

serendipitous textures. The colors varied among silver, gray,

orange, and black, with some evident traces of century-old paint.

We began construction by laying the floor with the widest

planks one step up from ground level, and building a small

double-door entry that was secured with a vintage padlock

found years earlier at an antiques/hardware store. Sets of small

four-paned windows, some with original glass, that were

purchased from a local architectural recycling company fit perfectly

and matched the age of the barn-wood walls. The roof was laid with

aged corrugated metal to secure it from the heavy northern California

rains. To reflect its connection with the countryside and to signify its

aged character, we added an eight-foot turn-of-the-century canvas canoe

to the top of the roof. A short pebble path was laid to link the cabin

with the garden, and, after just one rain-soaked winter and warm spring,

the flowers and vines that had been planted a single season earlier

had completely intertwined with the cabin as if it had been there

for the entire century.

Though no larger than a 200-square-foot room, the cabin was furnished

with a twin-sized circa-1900 wrought-iron bed, adorned with blankets

*Reminiscent of the English countryside, this front entry boasts
a rounded doorway painted in a bold crimson. The patio
table is covered with a 1930s table linen, and the basket, pail,
and flower container are from the 1940s.*

A pale yellow guest room includes a vintage cupboard and writing desk, both in rich shades of red. The vintage embroidered pillow with the profile of an American Indian accents one down-filled club chair, while an old trade blanket accents the other.

The brazen use of red directs the eye from the neutral walls to the living space.

Primitive checkerboards are illuminated by using outside light fixtures. A

fabulous 1920s dog painting framed in old-house lumber takes center stage.

from an early-twentieth-century Pullman railroad car and

custom ticking pillows. Placed nearby were a twig chair and

small handcrafted table. The walls were decorated with primitive

oil paintings from the early twentieth century, original oil-burning

lamps were hung from the eight-foot ceiling, and the floor was

accented with a seventy-five-year-old hooked rug. A stitched

forty-eight-star American flag was hung against the back wall as

a reminder of the source of inspiration from which the cabin

came. Since the vignettcs in the cabin changed from season to

season, it served as an inspiration to visitors seeking to capture

the Camps and Cottages style within their own homes.

The whimsy of lighted wooden flowers brightens an old florist's sign in this sitting room.

New England Colors

With the tranquility of Maine's historic Sebago Lake at her

doorstep and the powerful swales of the great Atlantic Ocean

at her back, Carol Bass, the creative genius behind Maine

Cottage Furniture, has styled her home in the colors she uses

in her critically acclaimed furniture. Reflecting on the nature

of cottage living, she says, "Upon entering a camp or cottage...

all our defenses fall away. We are returned to our childhood as

fresh beings and are drawn as close to the natural world as one

can be. In this setting our lives may be lived with sincerity and

without speed, as well as with tenderness, and without the

Making a color statement, another
guest room is furnished with the
simplicity of a white bed frame and
three-drawer cabinet, both from the
Maine Cottage Collection and set
against colorful walls.

Utilizing her dramatic taste for color, Bass has decorated her kitchen area in contrasting blue and green, influenced by the Maine sky and the lake's water.

© 2001 Maine Cottage
Furniture/Dennis Welch

tensions of the modern workplace. In a cottage setting, tenderness and thoughtfulness abound." She

designs her furniture in a manner consistent with the way in which she lives, and it is this mating of

vocation with avocation that has provided her with such an exciting following.

"The furnishings in cottages have always intrigued me," said Bass, "because of their simple and humble

lines. I feel obliged to reflect the qualities of that simple lifestyle in the design and creation of each of

my pieces. They are uncomplicated and somewhat in tune with Shaker simplicity, yet they exist in a

design space accentuated with the radiance of color. I feel that color and form represent direct con-

nections to one's soul, not unlike music and poetry. In choosing to be surrounded by sensuous colors

we are able to make our life journey more robust and meaningful."

The salmon shutter bed adds a perfect touch to this children's bedroom, especially as a contrast against the red-oak flooring.

Heartland Memories

While growing up in central Illinois's Knox County, midway between the Mississippi and Illinois Rivers, designer Steve Reed was surrounded by cabins and cottages, both rustic as well as fine-hewn. Combine that with the fact that the area has always been home to some of America's most respected antiques dealers and you can understand why Reed immersed himself in the study and observation of the architectural and crafts history of his immediate hometown, as well as the picturesque countryside stretching between St. Louis and Chicago. Upon relocating years later to the San Francisco Bay Area, he brought

"The Z shutter, though common in the Midwest, has always cried out for color and adaptation," Reed notes. "I softened the corners, accentuated the Z, and washed the whole thing in a deep buttercup yellow. I'm pleased with the way it has worked." For Reed it is another wonderful makeover of a heartland memory.

Steve Reed has created his own style of garden furniture that is comfortable standing alone or outfitted with tartan cushions. The sea-foam green color not only makes a statement among the garden plantings but provides a notable contrast to the nearby hothouse with its vivid red outline. Bold homemade colors are a Steve Reed hallmark.

with him the best of the heartland and combined those traditions with the colors and excitement that he discovered within the forests and upon the shores of the Pacific Ocean. Living in a turn-of-the-century clapboard farmhouse—one of the oldest surviving structures in the bayside town in which he now resides—he has elected to minimize structural changes, instead accenting the property, including a sizeable country garden, with appointments and furniture crafted in his work space that is also located on the property. From there he operates Steve Reed Painted American Country Furniture. His love of color abounds throughout his "work in process" and is an exciting example of the way in which one can transform an otherwise plain canvas into a bright and airy cottage.

True Blue

A native of Nebraska, textile designer and purveyor Sidney Muncy has

magically transformed the interior of her 1970s suburban California

home into a spectacular cottage with the look, feel, and warmth

of the 1930s. It is one of the finest examples of what creativity and

determination can do for the newest of homeowners, even when

faced with the daunting task of breathing color and life into a world

of whites and neutrals. Seasoned by years of design experimentation,

she has parlayed her ingenuity and success into one of America's

leading lines of country textiles, Country House Fabrics, and in doing

so has inspired legions of others to transform their neutral living

spaces by using splashes of vintage colors and accessories.

A combination of vibrant colors and large,
well-spaced furniture pieces, including a
spectacular wide-planked antique dining
table, redirects the eye away from neutral
walls toward the activity associated with this
exciting country design.

Anchors aweigh! Pries's whimsical touch guided a local builder to turn these entryway windows into portholes, complete with authentic mooring rope. The lighting, vintage shutters, and magnificent pond boat are offset by wide-planked flooring and bead-board walls, giving it a true nineteenth-century Cutty Sark feel.

Seaside Trails

Mention "mobile" or "manufactured" home and most Americans, perhaps unfairly, envision a rusted

trailer sitting on concrete blocks and guarded by vicious dogs—unless, that is, you are architect Lynn

Pries and the home is tucked within a private seaside cove. Envigorated by a "beach home" project for

a successful couple, Pries—driven by the structure's unfettered ocean views from the front, and canyon

and trail views at its back—has transformed what was an uninspired manufactured living space into a

quintessential 1930s beach cottage where the most discerning critic would be hard pressed to detect

even a whisper of prefabrication. Employing bold outside colors, as well as wooden decking and

vintage park benches, the setting is a comfortable space for viewing surfers, sailboats, and magnificent

sunsets. Adorned in a vintage nautical theme, this "cottage" is yet another example of how a creative

designer or homeowner can transform the most mundane of living spaces.

California Colors

Constructed in 1939, this cottage represents one of stylist Becky Clarke's finest redesigns. Tucked into a corner lot along a narrow lane reminiscent of the English countryside, Becky and husband Jim discovered the uncharacteristic and drab stucco property in 1994. With the assistance of local builder and British expatriate Mike O'Neil, they jumped headfirst into a year-long remodel, removing portions of walls to reveal a view of the ocean. They also replaced all of the deteriorating aluminum window frames with custom wooden frames accented with fixtures shipped from central England. The plaster walls in each of the five rooms were repaired and given new life with coats of the boldest tones of greens, yellows, and salmons trimmed with white molding.

Quintessential eclectic defines this Camps and Cottages décor. The room is washed in a bright green and includes complementing styles of furniture. The two 1940s rattan chairs are from Hawaii, and the bench turned table sits on a piece from Utah's Rocky Mountain Rag Rug that was woven from remnants. The three lamps surrounding the couch are distinctly nautical. One was handcrafted in Massachusetts and depicts a clipper ship, one portrays the end of a sports pier complete with the day's catch hanging from a rail, and the third is a British adaptation of a 1930s wooden cruiser. Atop the bench in front of the couch is a large 1940s handcrafted tug complete with engine below deck.

This particular shade of green in this dining area, as well as many of the other interior colors, was created by matching a color on a map linen from the 1930s. The green shelving provides a dramatic backdrop for this collection of old hotel silver and boating cups as well as a medley of trophies, paintings, and handcrafted boats, all from the 1920s and 1950s.

The front of the home, which faces the ocean, was

reconfigured by adding wooden bay windows in the breakfast

area and a railed front porch accessed by a wall of French

doors linking it to the front living room. The courtyard living

room was transformed with the introduction of two complete

walls of French windows, providing a tranquil view of

the courtyard garden.

The outside colors are a blend of British red, forest green, and

white, and, as is typical with British cottages, the front door is a

bold yellow. The home's lawn and gardens—which previously

did not have any significant landscaping—were improved by

This creative use of an "outhouse" for a garden shed adds character to this garden landscape.

adding large trees, roses, and more than forty other varieties of

flowers and bushes. Ivy was planted along the entire side wall

fronting the country lane and, in just two growth seasons,

enveloped the area as if it had been present for the entire life of

the home. Colorful window boxes were hung under each window

and planted with hanging foliage that is changed each season. As

a final touch, the property was ringed with a short white picket

fence, through which all of the foliage has grown, providing it

with a lived-in patina. This home, a feature of its local "Charm

Tour," stands out as an illustration of the creative use of color and

is one of the best examples of the Camps and Cottages style.

This living room, painted a cheerful buttercup yellow, is furnished with 1920s club chairs upholstered in a rugged Ralph Lauren floral fabric, a vibrant red cupboard, a salvaged coffee table, a vintage hooked rug, a 1920s mirror from the Adirondacks, and early landscape paintings.

Salt Air

This classic cottage, built in 1928, features a New England

design. Owners Judi and Luck Patterson have built a nautical

theme around this design. Characterized by a pale-pink wood-

shingled exterior reminiscent of Cape Cod, visitors are

immediately transported to the Pacific as they enter the living

room with its hand-oiled redwood interior. The amber hue of

the hardwood flooring, redwood walls, and open redwood

beams provide a magnificent backdrop for the inclusion of

Another view of the bedroom reveals
an oversized election sign from rural
Illinois and a basket of colorful
1930s cotton trade blankets.

149

original stained-glass windows, seafaring equipment, vintage pond

boats, primitive oil paintings, and classic signs. With the cottage stand-

ing much as it did in 1928, including solid-wood construction without

a stitch of concrete, the owners have carefully chosen vintage pieces

that provide patina and warmth while working within the structure's

dimension and scale. Having been featured in a number of America's

leading home-design magazines, this seaside cottage is awash with

color and whimsy. Its soulful and talented owners have seen to it that

the cottage continues to represent the very best in creative cottage design.

Original redwood extends throughout the house, including the kitchen area. "Though the kitchen and breakfast area is compact, the wall of windows provides a widening effect and makes it a consistently favorite room of the cottage," says owner Judi Patterson.

This living room and dining room are wallpapered in red gingham. The dining room plays host to an antique pine table encircled with vibrant chairs.

Liberty Cottage

Tucked into the heart of old Carmel, California's most admired seaside community, the owners have named their home "Liberty Cottage" and have chosen to dedicate the styling of its interior to Old Glory.

Constructed in the 1920s by M. J. Murphy, one of Carmel's most prolific builders of that period, the home is characterized by its high-beamed ceilings, planked hardwood flooring, and arched doorways.

Styling throughout the house is characterized by a blend of Cape Cod and central coast country, as well as the owners' own creations. Baskets, carefully designed from old techniques and original New England templates, abound in almost every room, and handfuls of weathered concrete figures provide a perfect fusion of east and west.

Vintage

Once the basic bones of a living space have been designed,

colors selected, and anchor pieces introduced, the

excitement of establishing a home with lived-in warmth

begins. From the Camps and Cottages perspective, this is

the stage where style and whimsy come together. Though

there is no right answer to the question "What's the best

way?" there are a few things to keep in mind.

Sock monkeys are the epitome of whimsy and add warmth to any cottage or cabin.

Vintage dinnerware and hotel silver adorn the shelves of cottage kitchens and dining areas.

Family History

First and foremost is the focus on family. To the extent that

family photos, art, and mementos are available, they should be

displayed and interwoven with the space's anchor pieces to

link past and present. This does not mean overwhelming the

space with all of the items from Auntie Mame's closet, garage,

and cellar. It means carefully placing select items that mean

the most to you; these will provide a glow to the space.

Collections

If you are a collector of china, silver, pillows, and so forth,

consideration should be given to highlighting the "best of

show" in a cabinet, upon a ledge, or along a bookcase for

appropriate attention, use, and effect.

Dolls remind one of childhood. Skookum dolls are classic collectibles of the American West.

159

Accents

Though the list of accents is infinite, including birdhouses, baskets, pots, shell boxes, signs, metal and wildlife trophies, a few deserve special mention due to their color, dimension, texture, and sense of whimsy.

Naive, Primitive, and Vintage Paintings

Between 1900 and 1940, American artists, schooled as well as self-taught, engaged in an explosion of landscape, seascape, and portrait paintings in both oil and watercolor. One could even subscribe to programs established by city art organizations that provided the subscriber, on a monthly basis, with original sketches produced by struggling artists. Though increasingly difficult to find, nothing infuses

There is nothing more dramatic than grouping certain items on a wall, fence, or table. The beauty of these vintage watering cans, flowerpots, and birdhouses is accentuated when displayed as a collection.

In 1911, author Harold Bell Wright wrote the novel The Winning of Barbara Worth. Four years later a group of investors hired architect R. M. Taylor to

design and build the desert region's only "big city" hotel and named it after the book's heroine. The Gorham Silver Company was commissioned to design the

hotel's silver, and the hotel owners instructed Gorham to inscribe each piece with the image of Barbara Worth from the book cover. Though the hotel was

destroyed by fire in the 1930s, its memory remains alive today on the face of the surviving silver pieces.

a cabin or cottage with more warmth and soul than the

introduction of those pieces to a cottage or cabin. Focus upon

the colors, message, and patina of the piece and not necessarily

upon its condition. Some of the warmest pieces that have gone

through the store required some back taping and frame repair.

Other than that, they are sold "as is" and remain in great demand.

Hotel Silver

Nothing captures America's golden era of travel more

captivatingly than the heavy silver teapots and silver services

that were used by America's hotels, railroads, and steamship

lines, many of which were proudly etched with the

establishment's name or logo. Though the pieces were, for the

most part, an amalgam of silver and nickel, they were designed

These elements illustrate how decoration and function can work together to turn a common space into a unique stopping point.

by respected silversmiths such as Gorham, International Silver, and Reed & Barton to endure the hard life of commercial use; today these pieces continue to remind us of an age in which trips were slower, events more formal, and dining luxurious.

Years ago, after discovering several hotel teapots at a flea market, I decided that my dinner parties would, from that point on, be graced with hotel silver. Not long thereafter, while rummaging through a store specializing in architectural remnants, I came upon a large milk-bottle box caked with mud and lawn debris, out of which poked the handle of a butter knife with the inscription "La Quinta." Knowing La Quinta to be the classic desert resort first established in Palm Springs in 1925 and still

*Vintage dinnerware and colorful
cookie jars adorn this cottage tabletop.*

Cast-iron doorstops were widely used between 1900 and 1940 and most contained colorful depictions. Open doors provide snug cottages and cabins with roominess, personality, and links to the country gardens and natural surroundings.

considered one of America's great getaways, I carted the box of mud off the premises for $1. After a

week of carefully digging through it, I discovered a complete seven-piece silverware setting for ten people.

Since polished to their original luster, all seventy pieces of this vintage set regularly adorn my dinner table

and never fail to evoke conversations.

Vintage Matchbooks and Ashtrays

Though smoking is socially distasteful in many realms, its remnants are colorful reminders of past

events associated with adventure, mystery, and travel. Several years ago, while antiques hunting in New

York, my husband came upon a 1930s wooden card table decoupaged with sixty- and seventy-year-old

matchbook covers depicting the intriguing logos of restaurants, lounges, hotels, and roadhouses from

New York to San Francisco. It was a spectacularly colorful piece of folk art that was eventually sold to a couple in San Francisco to be used as a wall hanging. They collapsed the legs and hung the piece above a stone fireplace in their vintage cabin at Lake Tahoe. In the same manner, noted Berkeley artist Wanda Pettler has accumulated an intriguing collection of copper cowboy-hat ashtrays, circa 1930–40. Says Pettler, " My collection provides me with a warm reminder not of smoke-filled rooms but of the small and independently run roadside inns where one might have found them. They were the mom-and-pop places where families, exhausted from completing a full-day's leg of a summertime road trip, sought comfort, refuge, and a home-cooked meal."

A carved bear makes this turn-of-the-century horsehair brush a distinctive addition to any powder room.

Textiles

As accents, textiles may take a variety of forms, from blankets to rugs to hanging tapestries. Perhaps the most colorful, whimsical, and camplike are embroidered tourist and school pillows, as well as stitched tourist pennants and school banners.

Pillows, blankets, and baskets are cottage mainstays. They provide color and warmth and may be styled in virtually every room of the house. Here embroidered pillows sit atop a camp blanket from the Pan Pacific International Exposition held on Treasure Island in San Francisco in 1915.

Pillows

Long before the advent of the Internet and electronic media, leisure time for women often took the form of sewing bees and quilting sessions. Creating an embroidered pillow was a unique way to express a greeting to a family member or loved one hundreds of miles away or to remember a recent trip out West or back East. The messages were as simple as " I Love You" and "My Country," but in every instance they reflected intriguing modes of script, attention to detail, and multiple levels of color. Though difficult to find, these handcrafted items represent one of the warmest and most colorful accents for a cabin or cottage.

This collection of a herd of 1940s copper horses reflects the owner's passion for riding.

Embroidered pennants and banners, found in cottages, cabins, lodges, and university dorm rooms between 1890 and 1950, are harder to find than their airbrushed counterparts. They can provide color and excitement to a den or bedroom in a city home or to the rustic main room of a vacation retreat.

Pennants and Banners

Between 1900 and 1950 one never journeyed anywhere without returning with a tourist pennant. It

was very difficult to find a camp cabin, prep-school room, or college dorm room that didn't have the

occupant's graduation-class banner or travelogue tacked to the wall or affixed to the dresser. Though

many were custom crafted by groups or auxiliaries on home sewing machines, most were

manufactured by a host of companies, including Chicago Pennant Company, Vermont's Green Mountain

Studios, Ohio's Schloss Company, and Fisch Company of Los Angeles. The earliest picccs, and today's

most-sought-after items, were constructed of the softest pure-wool felt. Those that have survived over

the years, often hidden in attic steamer trunks, contain magnificently detailed appliqués and beautifully

stitched lettering. Unlike their painted and silk-screened counterparts, their color, tactile beauty, and

historical significance make them one of the best examples of cottage and cabin living.

Resources

Stores

Blue Springs Alabama
369 East 17th Street #23
Costa Mesa, CA 92627
(949) 642-4201

Bungalow
1850 South Coast Highway
Laguna Beach, CA 92651
(949) 494-0191

Camps and Cottages
1231 North Coast Highway
Laguna Beach, CA 92651
(949) 376-8474
www.camps-and-cottages.com

Christa's Antiques
329 Marine Avenue
Bulboa Island, CA 92662
(949) 675-1492

Fairmount Antiques
7515 Fairmount Avenue
El Cerrito, CA 94530
(510) 526-7585

Filoli Gardens
86 Canada Road
Woodside, CA 94062
(650) 364-8300

Magnolia Creek
1057 South Coast Highway
Encinitas, CA 92024
(760) 944-7033

Melange Antiques
1235 North Coast Highway
Laguna Beach, CA 92651
(949) 497-4915

Mixed Pickles Antiques
1746 Shattuck Avenue
Berkeley, CA 94709

Prize
2361 San Pablo Avenue
Berkeley, CA 94703
(510) 848-1168

Prize
1415 Green Street
San Francisco, CA 94109
(415) 771-7215

Quail Country Antiques
1581 Boulevard Way
Walnut Creek, CA 94595
(925) 944-0930

Red Lodge Creek
259½ Arch Street
Laguna Beach, CA 92651
(949) 376-7969

Sisters Antiques
1250 Solano Avenue
Albany, CA 94706
(510) 528-8020

Tancredi & Morgen
7174 Carmel Valley Road
Carmel, CA 93923
(831) 625-4477

Tom Baker Antiques
5011 Soquel Drive
Soquel, CA 95073
(831) 479-4404

Twin Concepts
883 Santa Cruz Avenue
Menlo Park, CA 94025
(650) 322-8171

WaterLemon
405 Railroad Avenue
McCall, ID 83638
(208) 634-2529

Wild Goose Chase
105 W. Chapman
Orange, CA 92866
(714) 532-6807

Yankee Girl Antiques
328 Sir Francis Drake Boulevard
San Anselmo, CA 94960
(415) 460-0400

Furniture and Fabrics

Country House Fabrics
651 Via Alondra #709
Camarillo, CA 93012
(805) 482-2006

Maine Cottage Furniture
P.O. Box 935
Yarmouth, ME 04096
(207) 846-1430

Rustix
P. O. Box 6190
42112 Big Bear Boulevard
Big Bear Lake, CA 92315
(909) 866-2900

Found Images
824 Travis
Wichita Falls, TX 76301
(800) 295-7795

Rocky Mountain Rag Rugs
2306 Benchmark Circle
Salt Lake City, UT 84109
(801) 467-4006

Shady Lady
42 Diablo Circle
Lafayette, CA 94549
(925) 284-1877

Steve Reed Painted American Country
Furniture
5702 Jefferson Avenue
Richmond, CA 94804
(510) 233-4624
www.stevereedfurniture.com

West End Light
385 West K Street
Benicia, CA 94510
(707) 745-4150

Wilma Gilbert Pillows
590 Sterling Gilbert Road
Knob Lick, KY 42154
(502) 432-5389

Interior Design

Candra Scott and Associates
30 Langton Street
San Francisco, CA 94103
(415) 861-0690

Scott Polizzi and Associates
664 Hayes Street
San Francisco, CA 94102
(415) 487-9025

Artists and Galleries

Wanda Westberg-California Impressionist
1075 Mariposa Avenue
Berkeley, CA 94707
(510) 526-1844

Inns and Resorts

Lake of the Woods Mountain Lodge
and Resort
950 Harriman Route
Klamath Falls, OR 97601
(541) 949-8300

Manka's Inverness Lodge
P.O. Box 1110
Inverness, CA 94937
(415) 669-1034